RESEARCH TOOLS YOU CAN USE

How Do I Use a Database?

Laura La Bella

IN ASSOCIATION WITH

ROSEN
EDUCATIONAL SERVICES

Published in 2015 by Britannica Educational Publishing (a trademark of Encyclopædia Britannica, Inc.) in association with The Rosen Publishing Group, Inc.
29 East 21st Street, New York, NY 10010

Distributed exclusively by Rosen Publishing.
To see additional Britannica Educational Publishing titles, go to rosenpublishing.com.

First Edition

Britannica Educational Publishing
J.E. Luebering: Director, Core Reference Group
Mary Rose McCudden: Editor, Britannica Student Encyclopedia

Rosen Publishing
Hope Lourie Killcoyne: Executive Editor
Jeanne Nagle: Senior Editor
Nelson Sá: Art Director
Michael Moy: Designer
Cindy Reiman: Photography Manager
Amy Feinberg: Photo Researcher

Cataloging-in-Publication Data

La Bella, Laura, author.
How do I use a database?/Laura La Bella.—First edition.
    pages cm.—(Research tools you can use)
Audience: Grades 3 to 6.
Includes bibliographical references and index.
ISBN 978-1-62275-374-1 (library bound)—ISBN 978-1-62275-376-5 (pbk.)—
ISBN 978-1-62275-377-2 (6-pack)
1. Databases—Juvenile literature. 2. Information services—Juvenile literature. 3. Information retrieval—Juvenile literature. I. Title.
QA76.9.D32L33 2014
005.74—dc23

2014006299

Manufactured in the United States of America

Photo credits
Cover and interior pages (background) © iStockphoto.com/Kalawin; cover (inset from left) © iStockphoto.com/vm, lucky338/iStock/Thinkstock, Tyler Olson/Shutterstock.com; pp. 4, 6, 9 © AP Images; p. 7 David Joel/Photographer's Choice RF/Getty Images; p. 8 Andersen Ross/Blend Images/Getty Images; p. 11 Medioimages/Photodisc/Thinkstock; p. 14 Google/AP Images; p. 15 Baran Özdemir/E+/Getty Images; p. 20 Catherine Yeulet/iStock/Thinkstock; p. 22 Google and the Google logo are registered trademarks of Google Inc., used with permission.; p. 23 Alex Slobodkin/E+/Getty Images; p. 24 SpiffyJ/E+/Getty Images; p. 25 monkeybusinessimages/iStock/Thinkstock; p. 28 NASA/Freddy Willems, Amateur Astronomer.

CONTENTS

CHAPTER 1

What Is a Database?

Databases can hold a wide variety of information. This can include local, state, and regional police reports and terrorist tracking.

A database is a collection of information that is organized and stored on a computer. This information is also called "data," which is why the collection is called a "database." This data is organized in a special way, where information is interconnected. This means that each piece of data is related to others in some way. Users can easily find all the information on a particular subject. Databases can also search for data by categories called "fields."

Some databases store written data. Books, speeches, and other documents are examples of written data. Other databases store mainly collections of numbers. These databases may include prices, sports statistics, or personal spending and saving.

Information on a database can be added, changed, deleted, and **retrieved** by a user. Another way to use a database is to simply store information so that it can be used at a later time.

When it comes to computers, **retrieved** means finding and collecting information from a database.

TYPES OF DATABASES

There are many different kinds of databases. The largest databases are usually run by and used by government offices and schools. These hold information such as reports, phone numbers, addresses, and statistics.

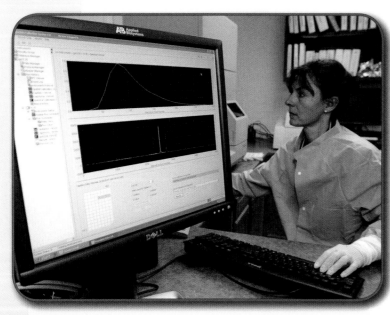

A forensic scientist uses a database to run a sample of DNA at a crime lab.

Commercial databases are also very large. They are used to conduct business online, known as e-commerce. Commercial databases help businesses keep track of information such as how many sales are made, prices, and the products they have in stock. These databases may also hold information on employees or customers.

Reference databases, such as those used by libraries, guide users to the location of information in books, magazines, and other publications.

Databases are housed on computers. These databases can help people gather, sort, and retrieve information.

Many of these databases can be used by the public for free. Many of these can also be found on the Internet.

Small databases can be created on personal computers for use by people at home. These types of personal databases let people store information and help keep it private.

Some of the most common databases used today are found in libraries. Library databases help people identify the type of books and information they need.

DATABASE USERS

Businesses and organizations have a great need for databases.

8

They are used by nearly every kind of organization imaginable. Libraries use them to organize the many different kinds of books they have. They also use them to track who has borrowed materials. Hospitals use them to store information about patients and their care. Police stations use them to track and record

Medical facilities use databases to track patient information and to order prescriptions that treat illnesses.

crimes. Banks use them to store information about finances.

Databases are also used by many different kinds of individuals. Students and office workers are just two examples of the types of people who rely on computerized information. Anyone who uses a computer, especially the Internet, has had some kind of experience with databases. Learning to use a database to access information is a useful skill that will benefit anyone throughout school and beyond.

CHAPTER 2

How Information Is Stored

Information in a database is stored as files. Think of computer files as electronic versions of actual papers kept in separate folders. In fact, computer systems use electronic folders to store files in a database. The information in files may be divided into records, each of which contains one or more fields.

These icons of folders on a computer screen open to reveal information saved within them.

RECORDS AND FIELDS

Records are smaller bits of information collected and stored in one place. A single article, report, or photograph is an example of a record. Each record contains one or more fields, which are the most basic units of data storage. Fields describe what is in a record, one piece of information at a time.

For example, a library database contains records of information about books and other materials it has

CLIENT TABLE

	FIELD 1	FIELD 2	FIELD 3
	Client ID	First Name	Last Name
RECORD 1	443	Jennifer	Roberts
RECORD 2	444	Dan	Smith
RECORD 3	445	Mark	Jones

Tables, like the one shown above, are used in databases to organize information.

How Information Is Stored

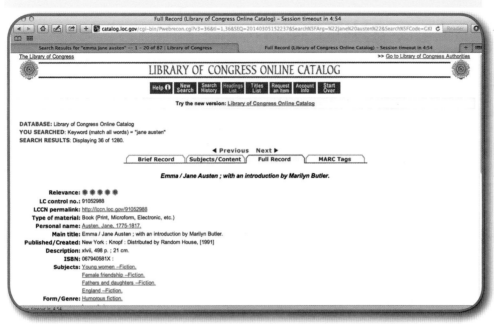

The Library of Congress Online Catalog stores thousands of pieces of information about books housed at the Library of Congress.

to loan. Fields within book records include the author's name, the book title, and the subject.

DATA WAREHOUSES

This Google data center, also called a warehouse, is where large-scale computer servers store millions of pieces of information. This information is accessed any time someone searches Google.com.

Sometimes separate databases are combined into one large collection. These large groups of databases are known as data warehouses.

Data warehouses contain data that has been collected over time. When information has

Large amounts of information can be retrieved from a data warehouse and analyzed to draw exciting new conclusions.

been moved from individual databases to a data warehouse, it can be analyzed, or searched to find patterns and trends. This allows users to gather a wider range of information about a subject than they could by searching each database separately. It also allows the original databases to continue operating and gathering data.

A **warehouse** is a large building where plenty of things can be stored together.

CHAPTER 3

How Information Is Organized

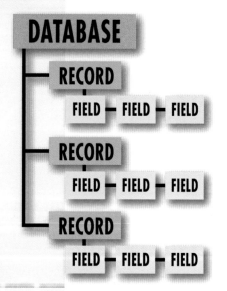

DATABASE
- **RECORD**
  - FIELD – FIELD – FIELD
- **RECORD**
  - FIELD – FIELD – FIELD
- **RECORD**
  - FIELD – FIELD – FIELD

Databases are made up of records and fields. Records describe information, and fields are sections of a record where information is stored.

Databases allow people to organize information in a way that helps them search for data. Regardless of which kind of database is used, information must be put in a certain order so that it is easy to retrieve the information from the database later on.

RELATIONAL DATABASES

Databases can be organized in various ways. The most common way is by data that is linked, or related. When information is organized this way, it is said to be in a relational database.

In this type of database, information is organized using tables made up of rows and columns. Each row is a record that holds certain information about one entry. That same type of information about other entries is held in other rows in the table. So the information is related, or linked, because it is the same type of data, even though it concerns different entries. This kind

Relational is a term that means connected, or related, to one another.

CLIENT TABLE

Client ID	First Name	Last Name
443	Jennifer	Roberts
444	Dan	Smith
445	Mark	Jones

ADDRESS TABLE

Client ID	Address
443	834 Sunset Avenue
444	213 Main Street
445	53 Elm Street

When data fields are linked and cross-referenced, a search can produce information from more than one database.

of organization of data allows users to sort through the information in a database to find exactly what they want.

CROSS-REFERENCING FOR EASY USE

Data fields can be linked together based on their relation to one another. When a database pulls related information from various fields, it is called cross-referencing. The organization of relational databases makes cross-referencing easy.

For example, in a search for "dog health" on the American Kennel Club website, any information in that database that has the words "dog" and "health" in it would show up on the computer screen. Users might find articles on dog fitness, healthy dog foods, trimming a dog's nails, or training tips. Fields that contain the search words are cross-referenced with other related fields so that any and all data about the health or fitness of dogs is found and shown to the user.

Edgar F. Codd was a mathematician who worked for the technology company IBM. Codd created the first relational database in the 1970s. He won many awards for his work.

CHAPTER 4

Getting Information from a Database

The majority of databases are kept on computers for easy access.

Organizing and storing information in a database is important. But users need to understand how to get information, or retrieve data, from a database so that the information can be used.

ASKING FOR INFORMATION

Users can retrieve data by asking the database to find information through a query. The most usual way a query is made is when a user enters words or numbers into a search box. The computer then searches

> A query is a formal way to search for information.

the database for records and fields that have the same words, terms, and numbers that were placed in the search box.

A search engine is a computer tool that allows users to query many databases on the Internet at once. For example, let's say a user wants to use a search engine to find information on Roald Dahl, the popular children's author. The

Two students research their class project by entering search terms into a database's search engine. More specific search terms will retrieve more useful information.

user would key (type) "Roald Dahl" into the search field. The computer would then search many databases for records or fields containing the words "Roald" and "Dahl."

KEEPING INFORMATION SAFE

Computer databases are an important source of information. They should be organized in such a way that retrieving that information is as easy as possible. However, there are times when data should be

Some databases contain very private information. Those databases must be secured to prevent hacking or theft.

hard to access. Some information found in databases is meant to be personal or private. Such data includes bank account information, Social Security numbers (Social Security is a system that continues to provide income for retired or disabled workers), and other information about a person's **identity**. Even letters written to a user's boss or friends could be considered personal data.

This kind of information needs to be kept safe. Database security then becomes an issue. Some databases are password-protected. Only users who know and key in the correct word or words are able to retrieve information in a protected database.

A common way to safeguard information is to have users log into a database with a password.

A person's **identity** is made up of everything that makes him or her special and different from others.

CHAPTER 5

Your Turn to Use a Database

Now that you understand databases and how they are used to organize information, let's practice how to use a database to conduct a basic search for information. For this activity,

Learning to use a database is a valuable life skill that will be helpful for years to come.

pretend your science teacher wants you to write a report on a planet. You are expected to explain why you chose this planet and to share detailed information about the planet with your class.

Start by going to the website of the National Aeronautics and Space Administration, or NASA (http://www.nasa.gov). You will want to search the NASA database. Query the NASA database for information on a planet

The NASA website (www.nasa.gov) contains a wealth of information about space and our solar system.

that interests you. When you key the planet's name into the search box and hit return, a list of articles about that planet will appear on the screen.

AN EXAMPLE

Suppose you are interested in Jupiter. Keying "Jupiter" in the search box brings up many articles, images, and videos about Jupiter.

By exploring database information about Jupiter, we learn that Jupiter is the largest planet in our solar system. More than 1,000 Earths would fit inside Jupiter. It is made up of helium gas and hydrogen gas, just like the Sun. Jupiter has at least 50 moons and a faint ring system.

LESSONS LEARNED

Following the Jupiter example, what can you learn about the planet that you selected? Can you use this and other databases to answer the following questions?

• How far away from the Sun is this planet?

Galileo Galilei was the first person to observe Jupiter with a telescope. He also discovered four of its moons.

- Does it have any moons?
- What is it made up of?
- When was it discovered?
- How has it been explored?

data Information that is created and stored in a computer.

delete To get rid of or erase, using a computer.

e-commerce Buying and selling goods over the Internet.

field The most basic unit of data storage.

record A grouping together of information.

register A place where official information on a place or person is gathered and kept.

related Connected in some way.

security The act of being kept safe.

statistics A collection of numbers and measurements.

BOOKS

Aboff, Marcie. *Analyzing Doggie Data* (Data Mania). Mankato, MN: First Facts, 2011.

D'Anna, Cindy. *Field Day!: Represent and Interpret Data.* New York, NY: Rosen Classroom, 2013.

Drew, Jon. *Matt's Field Day: Represent and Interpret Data.* New York, NY: Rosen Classroom, 2013.

Moore, Phillip. *How Can You Use a Computer?* Mankato, MN: Three Crows Media, 2013.

WEBSITES

Because of the changing nature of Internet links, Rosen Publishing has developed an online list of websites related to the subject of this book. This site is updated regularly. Please use the following link to access the list:

http://www.rosenlinks.com/RTYCU/Data

Index